The Turtle
and the Two Ducks

Animal Fables Retold from

La Fontaine

Patricia Plante and David Bergman

Illustrated by Anne Rockwell

THOMAS Y. CROWELL   NEW YORK

Library of Congress Cataloging in Publication Data

Plante, Patricia. The turtle and the two ducks.
Contents: The turtle and the two ducks—The horse
and the donkey—The wolf and the dog—[etc.]
1. Fables, American. 2. Children's stories, American.
[1. Fables] I. Bergman, David. II. Rockwell, Anne F.
III. La Fontaine, Jean de, 1621–1695. Fables. English.
IV. Title.
PZ8.2.P47Tu 1981   [E]   81-47409
ISBN 0-690-04148-9   AA CR2   ISBN 0-690-04147-0 (lib. bdg.)

1   2   3   4   5   6   7   8   9   10
First Edition

La Fontaine and His Fables

The fables of La Fontaine are one of the great treasures of French literature. Based on Aesop's legendary tales, La Fontaine's stories capture the charm, the humor, and the wisdom of the seventeenth century. This little book offers prose adaptations of the fables of La Fontaine's most beloved poems. They have been freely retold to capture both the irreverent fun of the original verses and his deep understanding of human foolishness.

Patricia Plante and David Bergman

The Turtle and the Two Ducks

"I am bored," thought the turtle to herself. "I want to go far away and see distant lands. Just because I have trouble walking doesn't mean I like staying at home."

The turtle told two ducks her troubles, and they thought of a plan that would please her.

"Do you see that road?" the ducks asked. "Well, the three of us will fly high above it on our way to America. We will see many lands and many people, and we will learn many, many things."

"Good!" cried the turtle. "When do we start?"

First, the ducks had to think of a way that the turtle could fly. They got her to bite into the middle of a long stick.

"Hold on tight," they told her, "and don't let go!"

Then each duck took an end of the stick in his beak. And the ducks flew into the sky and carried the turtle with them.

Everywhere people looked up to see the strange flying machine. No one had ever thought that a slow heavy turtle could fly so fast.

"A miracle!" cried the people. "Come see the Queen of Turtles flying in the sky."

"A queen! I really am a queen!" shouted the proud turtle.

Oh, the poor turtle! If only she had said nothing! Because when she spoke, she let go of the stick and fell all the way to the ground.

She broke into a dozen pieces right at the feet of the people who had watched in wonder. Parents turned to their children and said, "Look, now you see what happens when you talk with your mouth full!"

The Horse and the Donkey

Most animals learn while they are still young to help one another whenever they are in trouble. But a few animals never learn to help their neighbors.

Take this horse. He was traveling with an old tired donkey. But the horse was carrying nothing, and the donkey had four big boxes on his back.

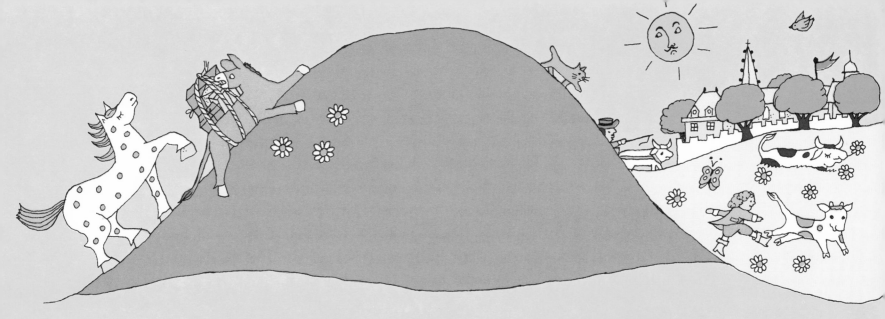

In the middle of a steep hill, the donkey fell down.

"Please help me," called the donkey to the horse. "If you don't, I'll never get these boxes to our owners in the city."

The horse pretended that he didn't hear and walked on a few steps more.

"Please help me," cried the donkey again. "I'm not asking much. You're so young and strong that if you carry two of the boxes you will not grow tired."

Still the horse wouldn't carry any of the donkey's packages. "Why should I do anything for a lazy old donkey?" he said. And he stood around until the donkey died.

But don't think the horse wasn't punished. Now he had to carry back to the city not only the boxes but the donkey too!

The Wolf and the Dog

A pack of wolves kept stealing food from the people of a small village. The people were very angry and bought watchdogs to scare away the wolves. The dogs were very big and mean. And in a few months the wolves got so little to eat that they became nothing but skin and bones.

One day a wolf was hunting for food, and he met a very large and beautiful dog. Because he was enjoying his walk, the dog didn't try to scare away the wolf. The wolf didn't try to frighten the dog either, because the dog was so much bigger and stronger. Instead, the wolf walked up to the dog and told him how nice he looked.

"Thank you," said the dog, "but you could look as nice if you wanted to. You wolves are stupid to stay out in the woods where you're alone and have nothing to eat and have to fight for everything, and no one ever throws you a bone. If you'll follow me, I'll show you a better way to live."

The wolf asked, "What will I have to do?"

"Very little," said the dog, "Just chase away strangers, play with children, wag your tail when your owners come home, and do whatever they say. Then they will give you meat and bones and a warm place to sleep."

Oh, the wolf was very happy. He began to dream of all the wonderful things he could have.

But then he noticed a cut on the dog's neck. "What's that?"

"Nothing," said the dog.

"What do you mean nothing?"

"Well," answered the dog slowly, "sometimes my owners tie me up with a rope, and the rope cuts me."

"You mean you can't go where you want?"

"Not always," said the dog. "But is freedom so important?"

"It is to me!" answered the wolf. "I would rather go without food than be without freedom." And with that, the wolf ran away.

The Fox and the Stork

Mr. Fox was very stingy. He hated to spend money on food. When he invited Miss Stork to dinner, he gave her as little to eat as he could.

He served her only soup. And first he took out all the meat and vegetables, so that the soup was as clear as water, and then he put the soup in a flat dish. Miss Stork with her long thin beak couldn't eat a drop. But Mr. Fox was able to gobble up all his soup.

Miss Stork was very angry. She wanted to punish Mr. Fox for his trick. And a few days later she invited him for dinner.

"Thank you, Miss Stork," replied the fox. "I always like visiting friends."

Mr. Fox arrived right on time for dinner. But Miss Stork was not ready. She made him wait and smell the delicious gravy cooking in the kitchen. She wanted the fox to grow very hungry.

When Miss Stork finally brought dinner to the table, the food was in long thin glasses, just right for her long thin beak. But hungry Mr. Fox couldn't get his big wide mouth close to the food.

He left Miss Stork's house without having eaten a thing. His long tail drooped sadly almost to the ground. He had learned his lesson, and he never tried to fool a stork again.

The Dove and the Ant

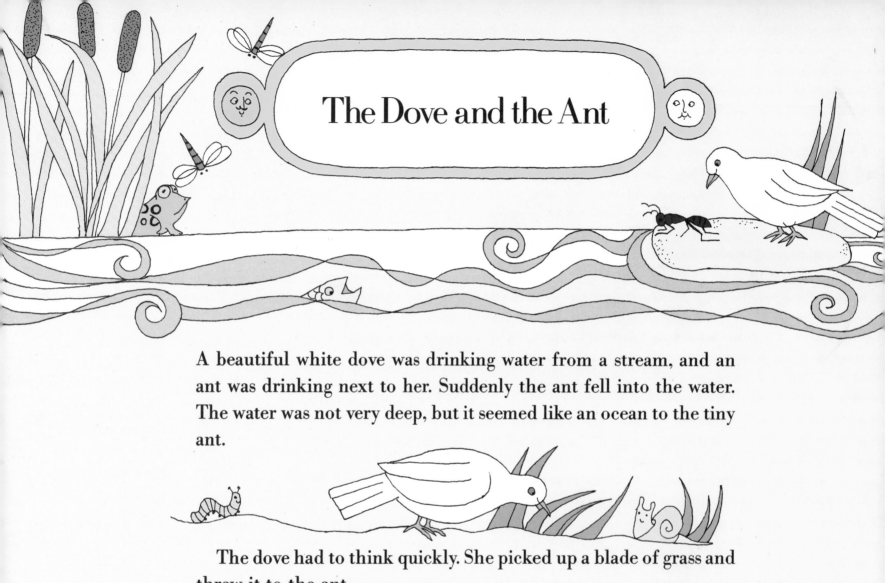

A beautiful white dove was drinking water from a stream, and an ant was drinking next to her. Suddenly the ant fell into the water. The water was not very deep, but it seemed like an ocean to the tiny ant.

The dove had to think quickly. She picked up a blade of grass and threw it to the ant.

"Grab on to the grass," called the dove, "and row it back to land."

The ant did as she was told and landed safely on the other side of the stream.

Just then a barefoot boy came through the woods carrying a bow and arrow. He was very hungry, and when he saw the beautiful white dove, he thought, "Wouldn't she make a delicious dinner."

The ant saw the boy raise his bow to shoot her friend the dove. Now it was the ant's turn to think quickly. She ran over to the boy and bit him on his foot so hard he jumped.

The dove heard the boy move, and she flew away, carrying along with her his dream of a delicious dinner.

Now this all proves a simple lesson: It's better to be smart than big.

The Turtle and the Rabbit

If you're going to finish first, you have to keep going. That's the lesson that the turtle taught the rabbit.

One day the turtle and the rabbit were talking in the barnyard.

"I'll bet you," said the turtle, "that I can reach that fence over there before you can."

"Before me?" answered the rabbit. "You've got to be kidding. Still I'll race you, if you want."

And so the rabbit and the turtle began to run.

But the rabbit soon stopped. He thought to himself, "I'm the fastest animal on the farm. I can run faster than the chickens or the donkey or even the dogs. I'm not going to tire myself out for this slow little turtle. Besides, no one will think I'm a good sport if I don't give the turtle a head start."

So the rabbit sat down and napped awhile and listened to the birds in the trees.

All of a sudden he saw that the turtle was almost to the fence. At once he dashed off. But it was too late. The turtle had won.

"You see, I was right!" laughed the happy turtle.

"But it wasn't fair!" cried the rabbit.

"Not fair?" asked the turtle. "Next time try racing the way I do—with your house on your back."

The Weasel and the Hole

Miss Weasel had been very ill. While she was sick, she ate almost nothing, and so she became very thin. But now that she was feeling better, she decided to give herself a treat and eat and eat.

She knew of a house where the people kept food in a little room. There was a small hole in the wall, and because Miss Weasel was so thin, she slipped right through the hole.

For a whole week Miss Weasel stuffed herself with cookies and crackers and beans and candy and nuts. Then she heard someone at the door.

She ran to the hole, but now she was too big to get through it. "Oh, I must be at the wrong hole," thought Miss Weasel, and she ran around the room looking for the right one. But soon she was back where she started. "Dear me, dear me," she cried. "What can the problem be?"

A rat, who had been watching her, had to laugh. "The problem, Miss Weasel, is that you've grown too fat. You came in thin, and you'll go out thin too—if you get out of this room at all. This is one hole you can't weasel out of!"

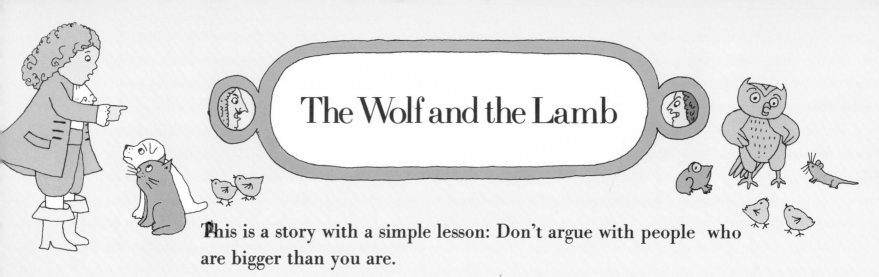

The Wolf and the Lamb

This is a story with a simple lesson: Don't argue with people who are bigger than you are.

The story begins with a lamb who was very thirsty and went to a nearby stream to drink from its cool clear water. Suddenly a wolf appeared.

The wolf was very angry, and he yelled at the lamb, "How dare you kick dirt into the stream and dirty my drinking water."

"Don't be angry," replied the little lamb. "I'm twenty feet away from you, and I haven't kicked so much as a single pebble into the water."

"That doesn't matter!" shouted back the wolf, coming closer to the lamb. "Besides, I know that last year you told lies about me."

"Oh, but, sir," answered the little lamb, "I wasn't even born last year."

"Well, if it wasn't you, it was your brother!" said the wolf, coming still closer.

"But, sir," explained the little lamb, "I have no brothers."

"Well, then, it was your father or your mother or your aunt or your uncle or one of your dozens of sheepish cousins. Somebody has been saying bad things about me, and it's time that I punished someone for those lies." By now the wolf was very near indeed.

And without another word, the wolf grabbed the lamb by his neck, dragged him into the forest, and ate him all up. And the lamb had no chance to finish the argument.

The Grasshopper and the Ant

All summer long, the grasshopper chirped. When the cold winds of winter came, she had nothing to eat. She had forgotten to store any food and did not have a scrap of a worm or a fly. Soon the grasshopper became hungry, and she asked her neighbor, the ant, to lend her some food.

"All I need is a few seeds," said the grasshopper, "or I'll die of hunger. You have my word as an animal, next summer I'll return everything I borrowed and more."

But the ant had worked hard. She did not want to give any food to the foolish grasshopper. So she asked, "What were you doing while we were gathering food?"

"Me?" replied the grasshopper. "Why, I sang for anyone who would stop and listen."

"Well," said the ant, "if you could sing *then*, you can dance *now*!" And she left the grasshopper to take care of herself.

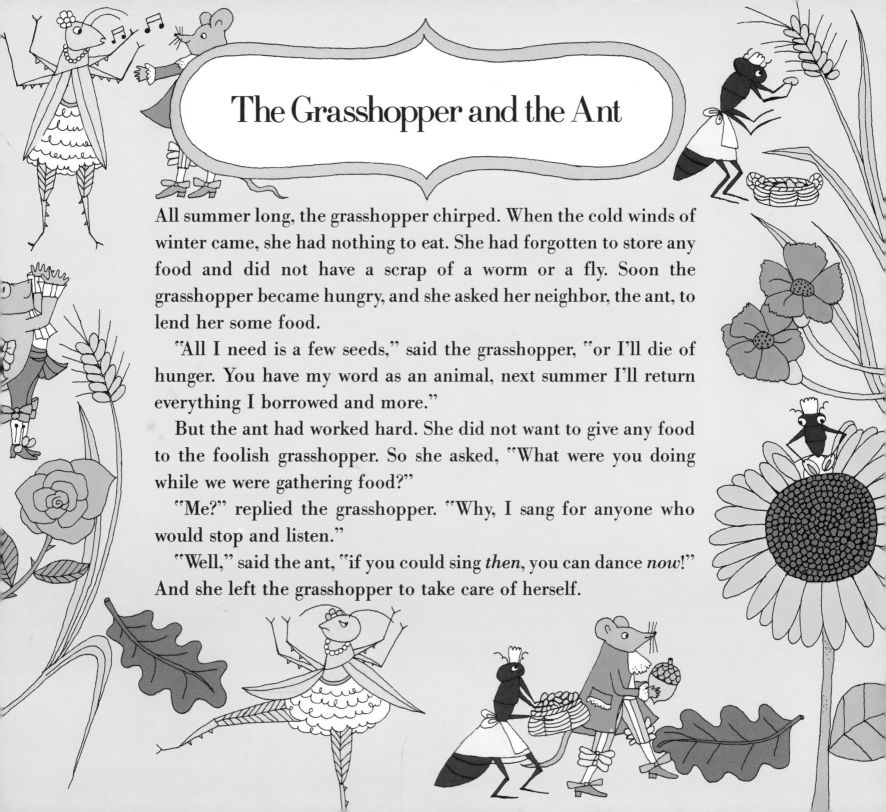

The Two Goats

Goats think only about two things—food and fun. Once they have eaten, they are ready to play. They like to run in the fields or to climb mountains.

One day two goats from two different villages decided to have some fun. They both went high up in the mountains.

By chance they met each other at a stream. The first goat stood on one side of the stream, and the second goat stood on the other side. Between them was a long piece of wood that a farmer had put there so he could cross the stream.

The goats also wanted to cross, but there was a problem. The piece of wood wasn't wide enough for two thin cats to pass each other, let alone two fat goats.

Each goat looked at the water. It was cold and deep and fast moving. Then the goats looked at each other to see who would go first.

But goats are very stubborn. Neither one would let the other cross first. They started walking across the board at the same time, and they found themselves nose to nose at the middle of the bridge.

They began to argue. "I should go first," cried one goat. "No, I should go first," cried the other. And they argued and argued until they both fell into the water and drowned.

The Fox and the Grapes

The fox was so weak with hunger, he could hardly stand up. Then he saw a grapevine hanging above him. The grapes were big and sweet and very, very purple. Oh, how the fox wished he could eat them! But he couldn't. The grapes were too high up, and he had no way to get to them.

So instead of wasting any more time, the fox told himself, "I was wrong. These grapes aren't any good. They're small and green and very, very sour. Only a fool would want them."

It wasn't true, of course. But would you rather have the fox sit around all day feeling sorry for himself?